EMELI SANDÉ

OUR VERSION OF EVENTS

ISBN 978-1-4803-6586-5

HAL•LEONARD®
CORPORATION
7777 W. BLUEMOUND RD. P.O.BOX 13819 MILWAUKEE, WI 53213

In Australia Contact:
Hal Leonard Australia Pty. Ltd.
4 Lentara Court
Cheltenham, Victoria, 3192 Australia
Email: ausadmin@halleonard.com.au

Visit Hal Leonard Online at
www.halleonard.com

HEAVEN

Words and Music by EMELI SANDÉ,
SHAHID KHAN, MICHAEL SPENCER,
HUGO CHEGWIN and HARRY CRAZE

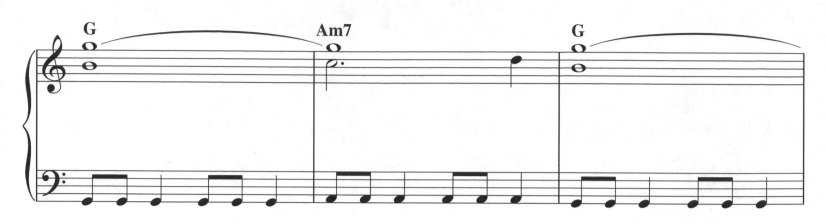

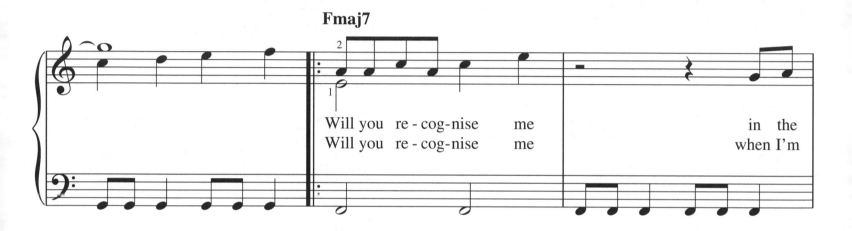

Will you re-cog-nise me in the
Will you re-cog-nise me when I'm

flash - ing lights? _ I try to keep my heart clean
steal - ing from the poor? _ You're not gon-na like me

but I can't get it right. ___
I'm noth-ing like be - fore. ___

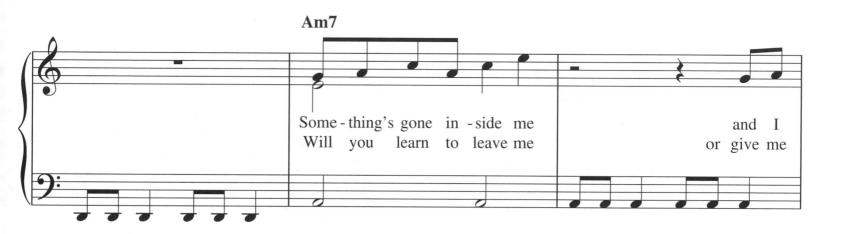

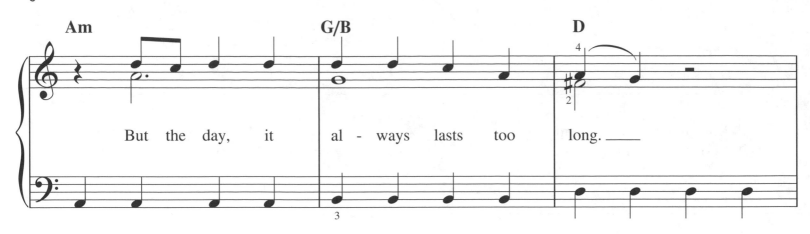

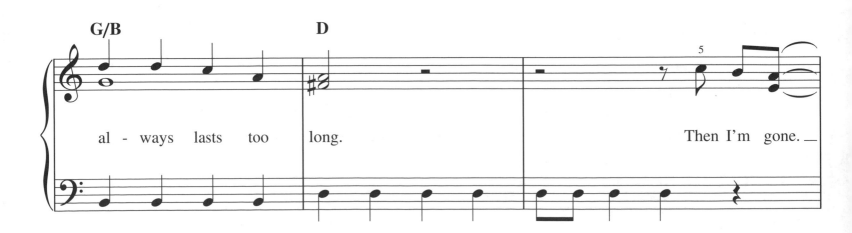

Then I'm gone. ____ Then I'm gone. ____ Then I'm

gone. ____ Then I'm gone. ____ Then I'm gone ____ Then I'm gone ____

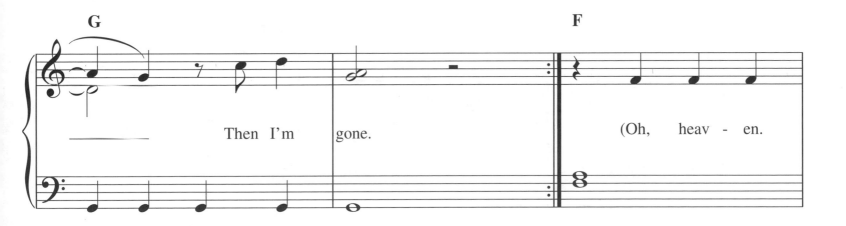

____ Then I'm gone.   (Oh, heav - en.

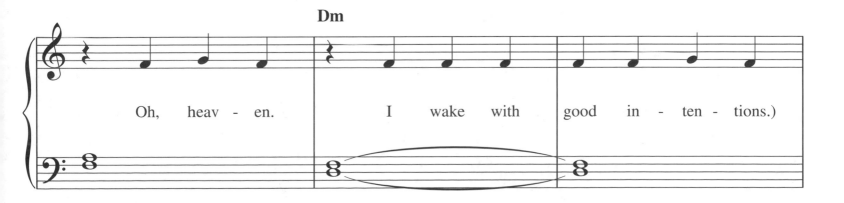

Oh, heav - en.   I wake with good in - ten - tions.)

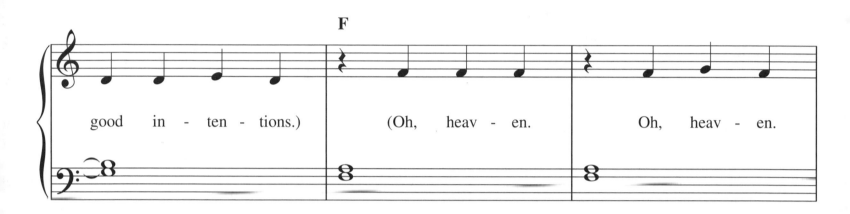

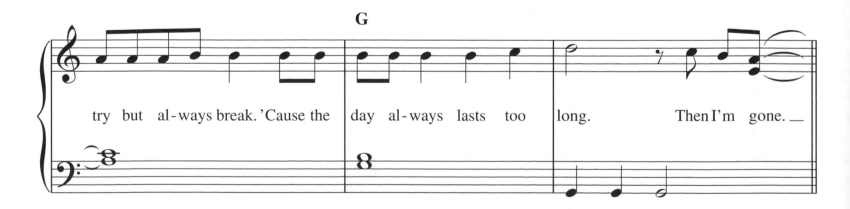

MY KIND OF LOVE

Words and Music by EMELI SANDÉ,
EMILE HAYNIE and DANIEL TANNENBAUM

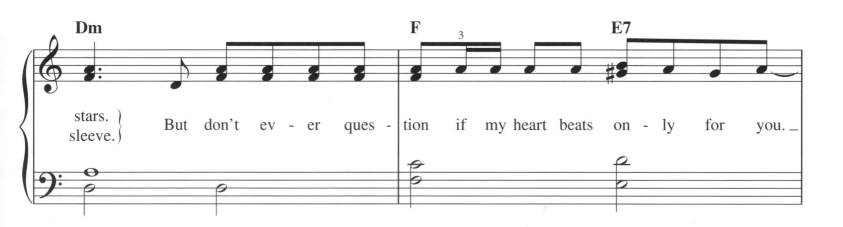

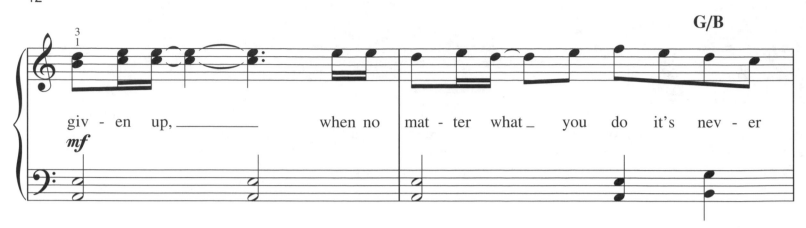

G/B

giv - en up, _____ when no mat - ter what _ you do it's nev - er

mf

C

good e - nough, _____ when you nev - er thought _ that it could ev - er

Dm

get this tough, _____ that's when

F **E7**

you feel my kind _ of _ love. _

Am

_ And when you're

G/B

cry - ing out, _____ when you've fall - en and __ can't pick your hap - py

C

off the ground. _____ When the friends you thought __ you had have - n't

Dm　　　　　　　　　　　　　　　　　　　**F**　　　　**E7**

stuck a - round, _____ that's when you feel my kind __ of __ love. __

1.

Am

14

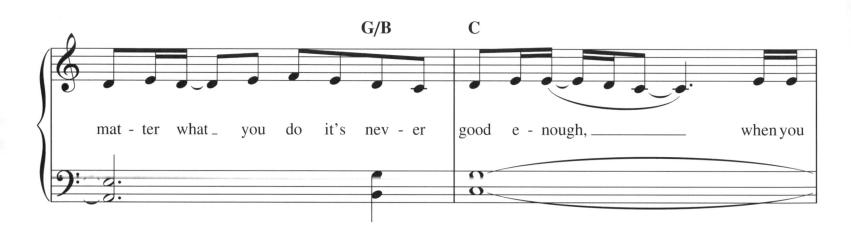

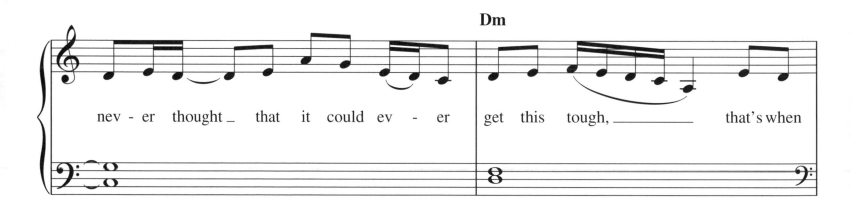

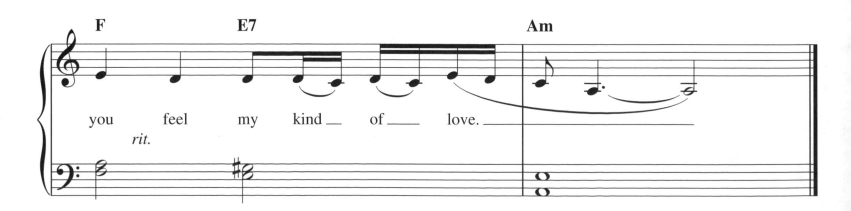

WHERE I SLEEP

Words and Music by EMELI SANDÉ
and SHAHID KAHN

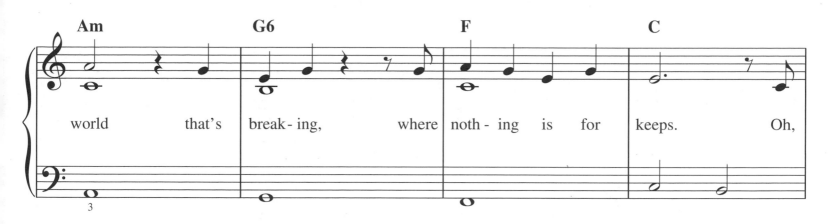

MOUNTAINS

Words and Music by EMELI SANDÉ,
SHAHID KHAN, MUSTAFA OMER,
JAMES MURRAY and LUKE JUBY

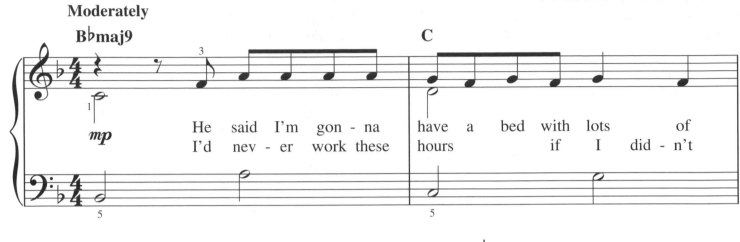

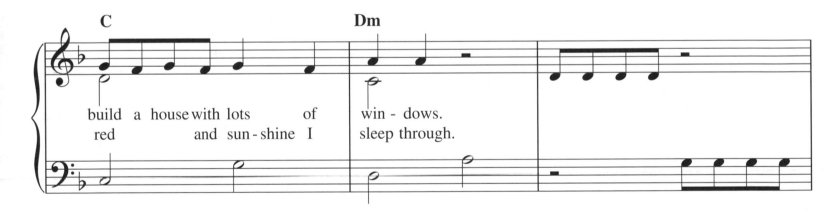

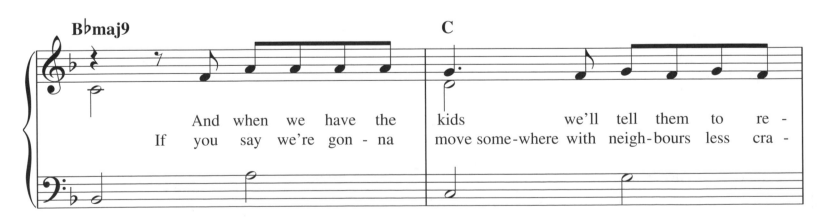

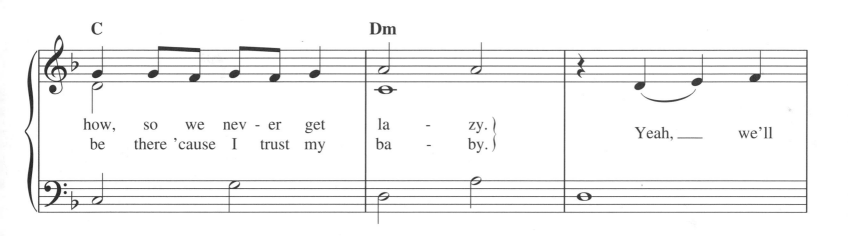

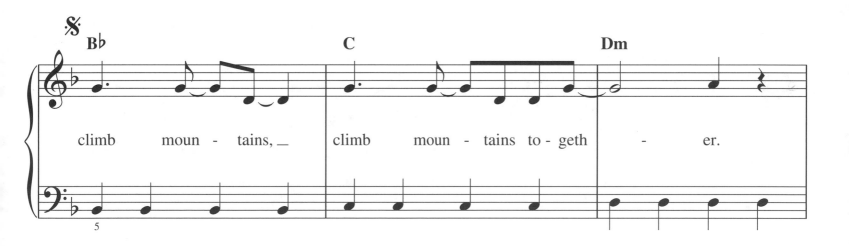

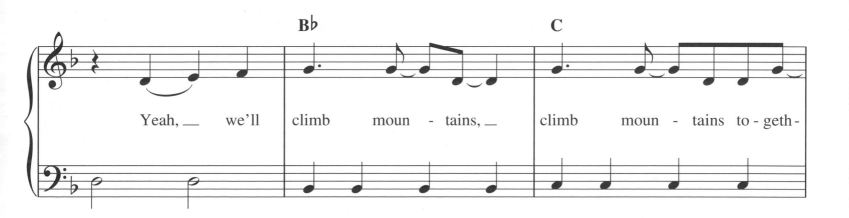

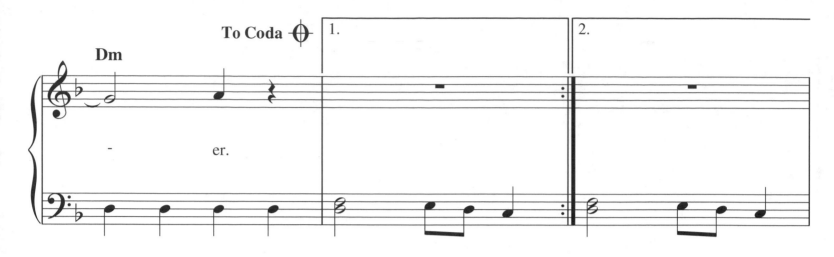

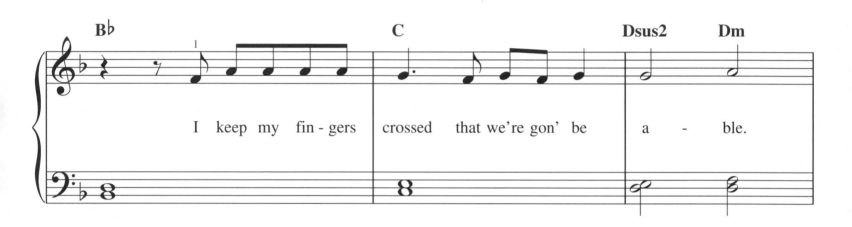

I keep my fin-gers crossed that we're gon' be a - ble.

I touch the wood for luck on our bro-ken

ta - ble. I know that it's our

heart that's gon - na save us.

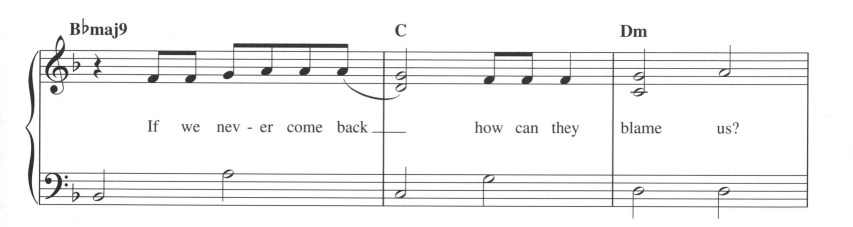

B♭maj9 **C** **Dm**

If we nev - er come back how can they blame us?

D.S. al Coda **CODA** **Dm** **B♭**

Yeah, _ we'll *mp* Yeah, _ we'll climb moun - tains, _

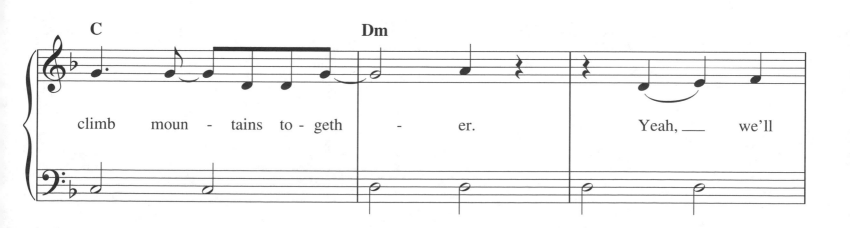

C **Dm**

climb moun - tains to - geth - er. Yeah, __ we'll

22

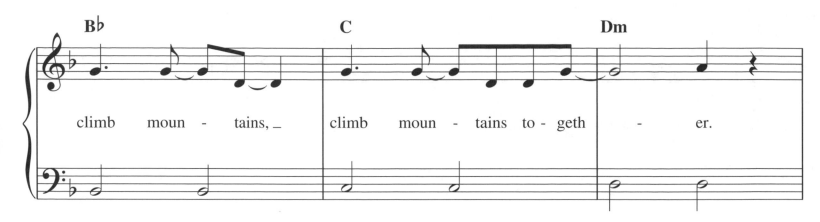

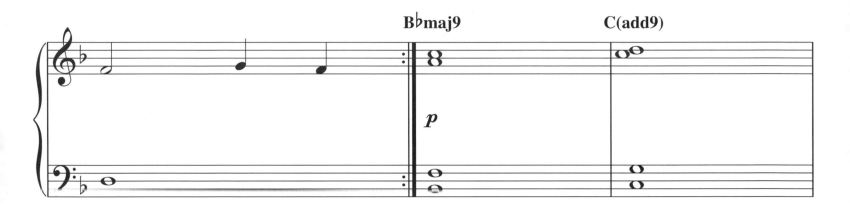

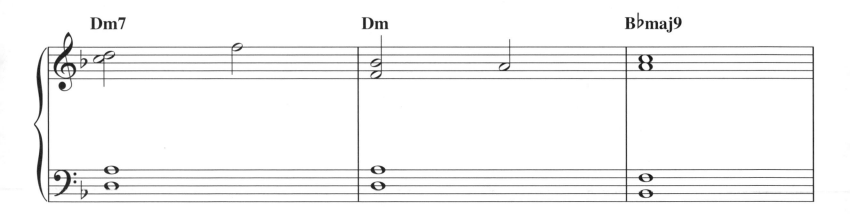

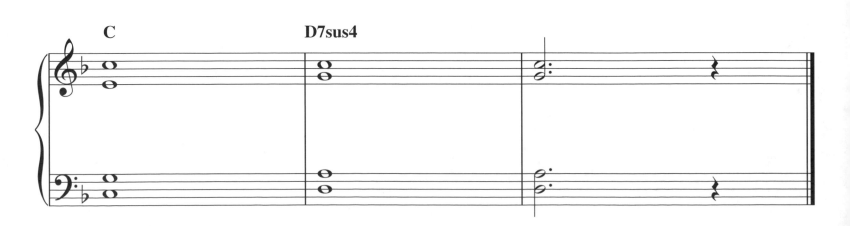

CLOWN

Words and Music by EMELI SANDÉ,
SHAHID KHAN and GRANT MITCHELL

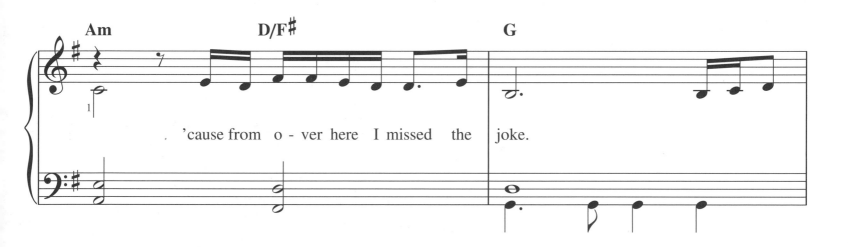

25

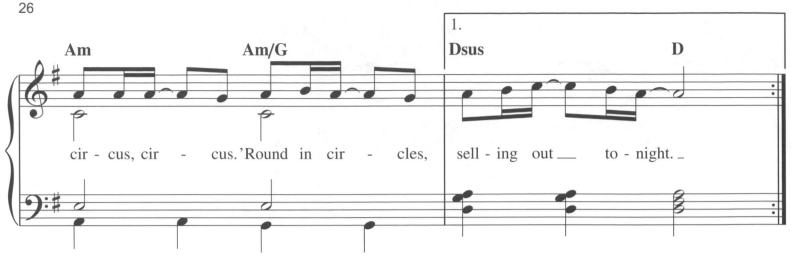

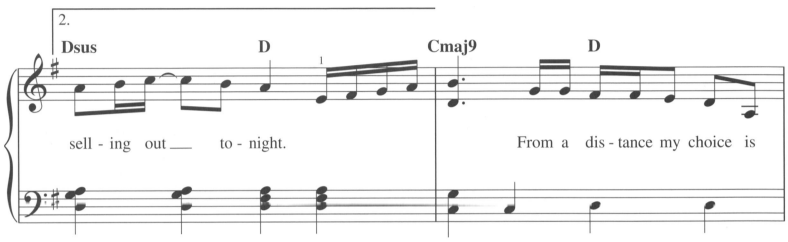

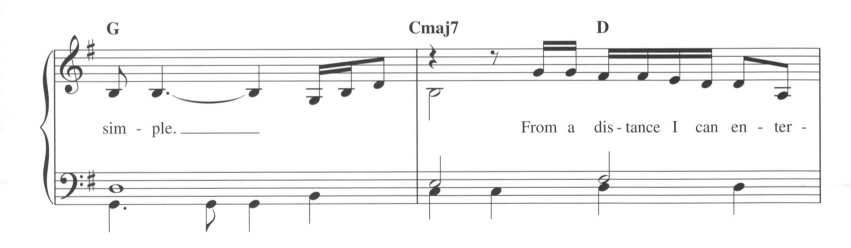

make-up on ___ my face. ___ But there's no way you can feel ___ it ___ from so

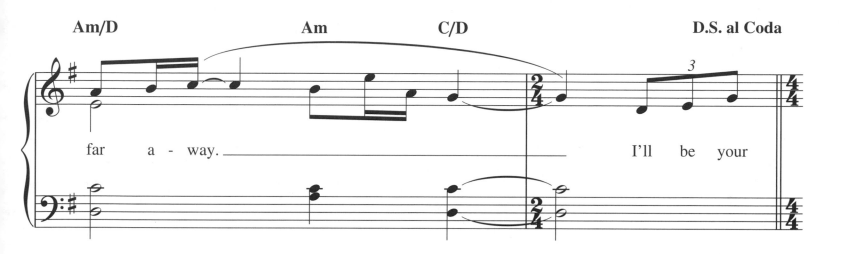

far a - way. ___ I'll be your

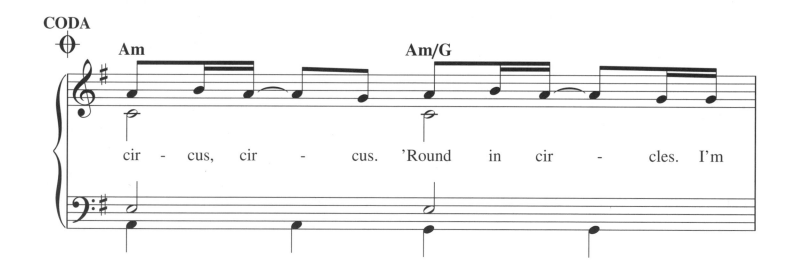

cir - cus, cir - cus. 'Round in cir - cles. I'm

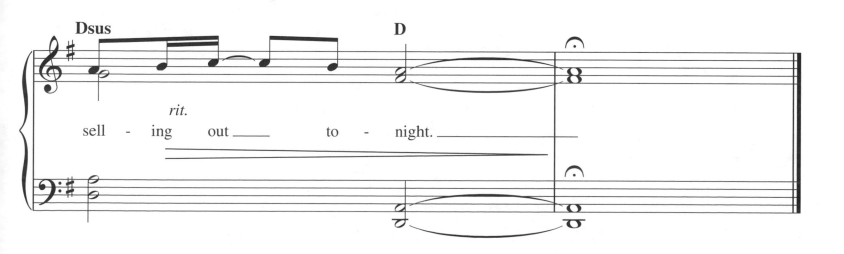

sell - ing out ___ to - night. ___

DADDY

Words and Music by EMELI SANDÉ,
SHAHID KHAN, MUSTAFA OMER,
JAMES MURRAY and GRANT MITCHELL

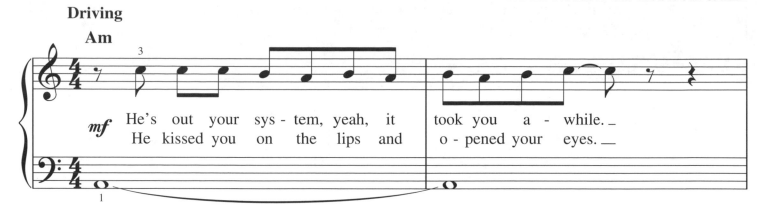

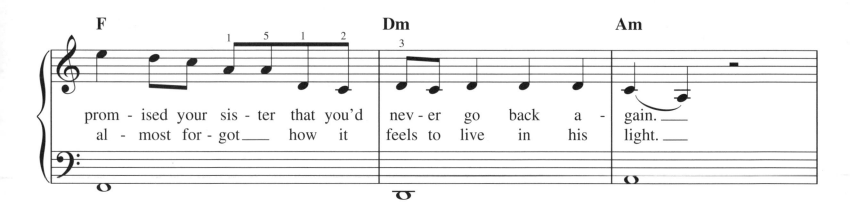

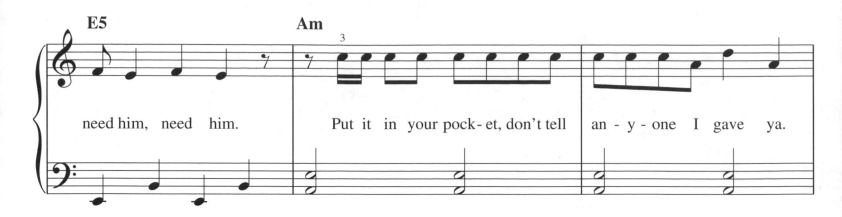

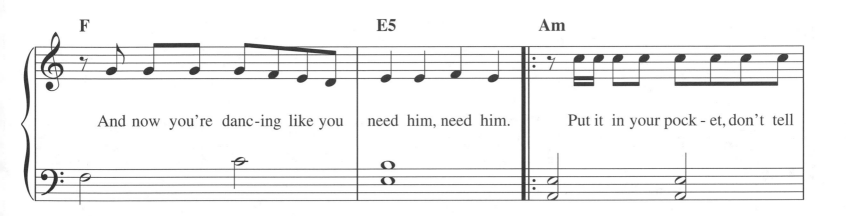

MAYBE

Words and Music by EMELI SANDÉ,
PAUL HERMAN and ASHTON MILLARD

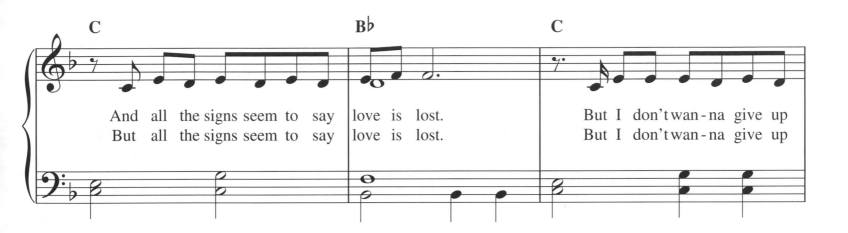

work. But may - be we should stop pre -

To Coda

tend - ing. We both know we're hurt - ing. May-be it's time __ to

Dm7 **C/E**

1. go. 2. go. May - be it's time __ to

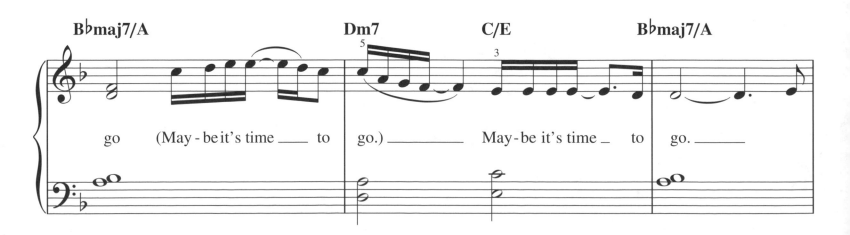

B♭maj7/A **Dm7** **C/E** **B♭maj7/A**

go (May - be it's time __ to go.) __ May-be it's time __ to go. __

SUITCASE

Words and Music by EMELI SANDÉ,
SHAHID KHAN, BENJAMIN HARRISON
and LUKE JUBY

Did-n't see it com - ing, no kind of warn - ing.
What changed so quick - ly? An - swer me! If you

I can't work out what I've done wrong.
must kill me at least please tell me why.

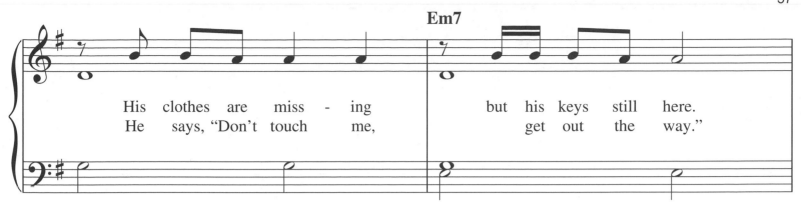

His clothes are miss - ing   but his keys still here.
He says, "Don't touch   me,   get out the way."

Please some-bod - y   tell me what's go - ing   on.
Will some - one tell me what's go - ing on to - night?

My ba - by's got a

suit - case.   He's tell - ing me it's too late.   But

don't no-bod - y, please don't ask __ me why.   'Cause all I did was

love ____ him, ____ but I can't stop him walk - ing. ____ My ba-by's got a

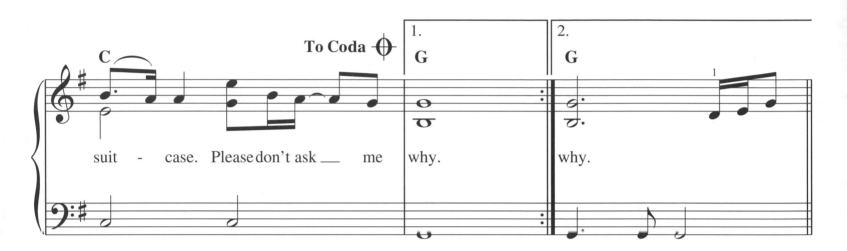

suit - case. Please don't ask __ me why. why.

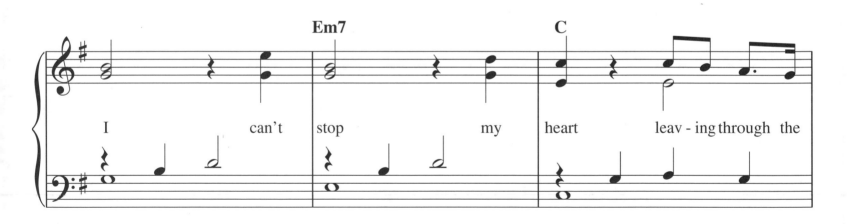

I can't stop my heart leav - ing through the

door. I can't un - pack my

heart 'cause he won't look at me an - y - more. _____ My ba-by's got a

CODA

why.

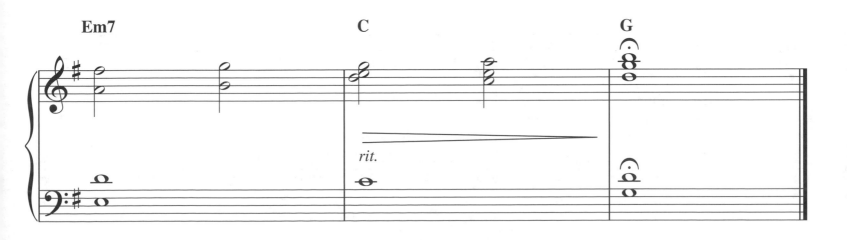

rit.

BREAKING THE LAW

Words and Music by EMELI SANDÉ,
SHAHID KHAN and BENJAMIN HARRISON

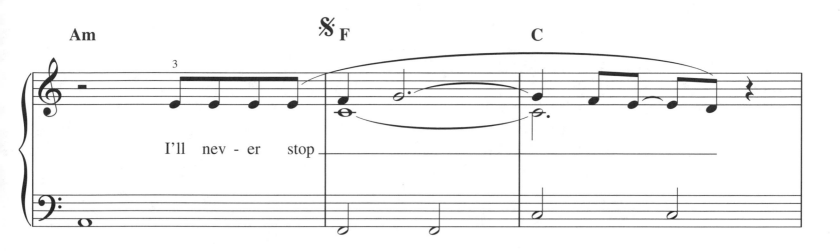

42

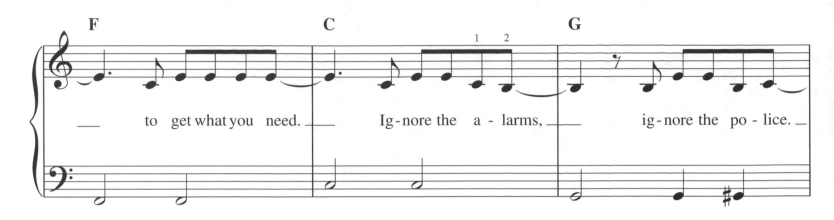

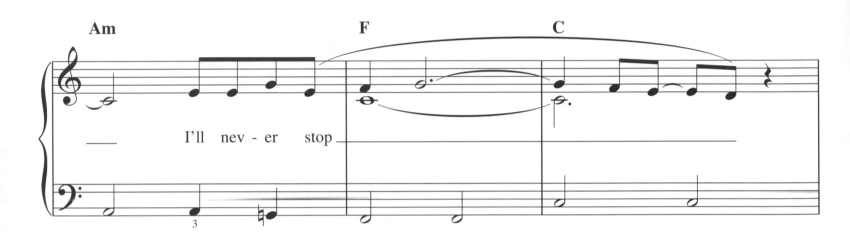

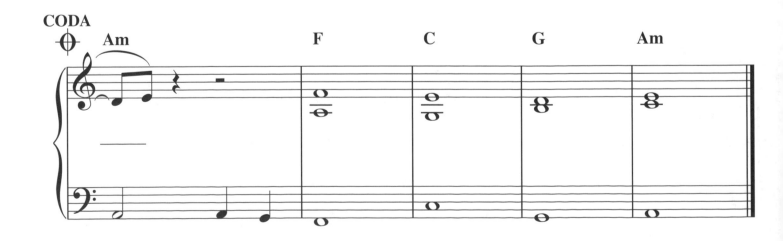

NEXT TO ME

Words and Music by EMELI SANDÉ,
HARRY CRAZE, HUGO CHEGWIN
and ANUP PAUL

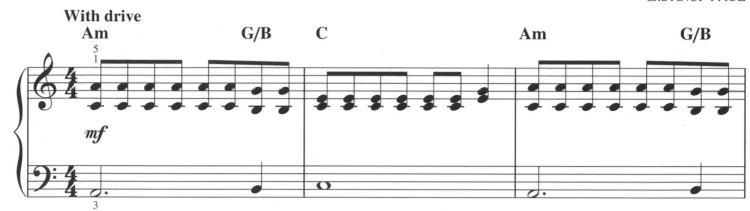

You won't find him drink-in' un-der ta-
mon-ey's spent and all my friends have van-

- bles,
- ished, and I can't
roll-in' dice and stay-in' out till
seem to find no help or love for

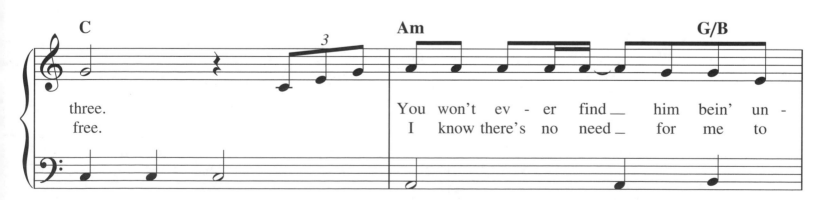

three.
free.
You won't ev-er find __ him bein' un-
I know there's no need __ for me to

faith - ful. You will find ____ him, you'll find ____ him next to me. ____
pan - ic, 'cause I'll find ____ him, I'll find ____ him next to me. ____

____
____ When the skies are grey and all the doors are clos -
end has come and build - in's fall - in' down ____

You won't find him try'n' to chase the dev -

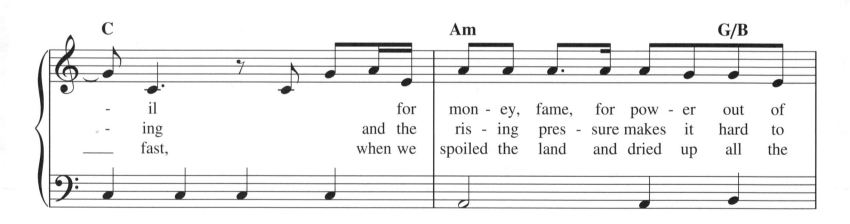

- il for mon - ey, fame, for pow - er out of
- ing and the ris - ing pres - sure makes it hard to
____ fast, when we spoiled the land and dried up all the

greed. well, all I You won't ev - er find him where the rest ____
breathe, need's a hand to stop the tears from fall -
sea, when ev - 'ry - one has lost their heads a - round ____

go. You will find ___ him, you'll find ___ him next to me. ___
-ing. I will find ___ him, I'll find ___ him next to me. ___
us, you will find ___ him, you'll find ___ him next to me. ___

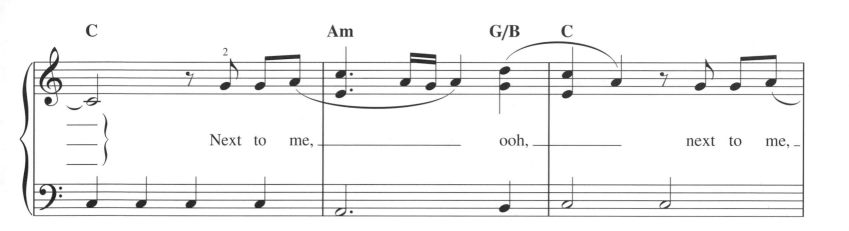

Next to me, _____ ooh, _____ next to me, ___

_____ ooh, ooh. Next to me, _____ ooh,

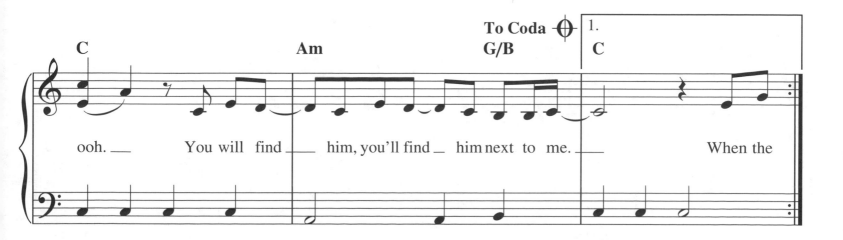

ooh. ___ You will find ___ him, you'll find ___ him next to me. ___ When the

2.

C

D.S. al Coda

CODA

C

When the

Next to me, —

Am   G/B   C   Am   G/B

ooh, _____   next to me, _____   ooh,

C   Am   G/B   C

ooh.   Next to me, _____   ooh, ooh,   you will find __

Am   G/B   C

__ him, you'll find __ him next to me. __

RIVER

Words and Music by EMELI SANDÉ
and SHAHID KHAN

If you're look-ing for the big ad -
want are ans - wers to your

ven-ture and gold is all that's on your mind. If all you
ques-tions and you can't seem to find no love for free. If you're

48

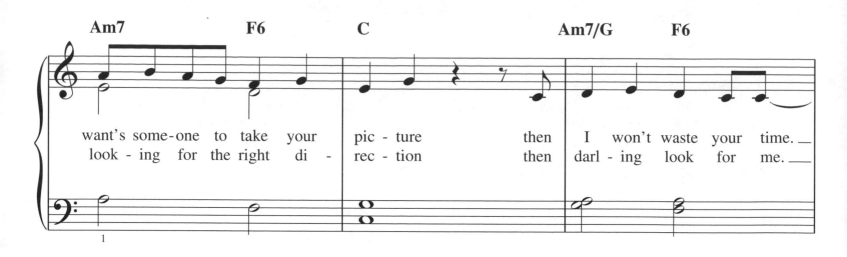

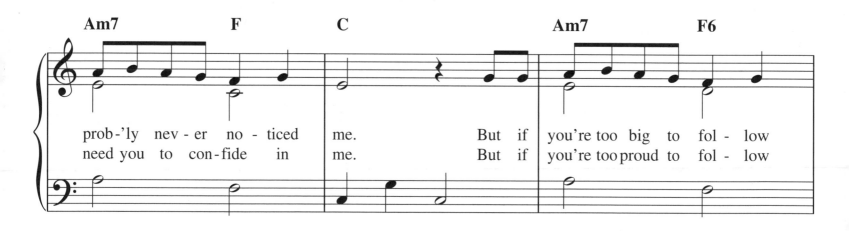

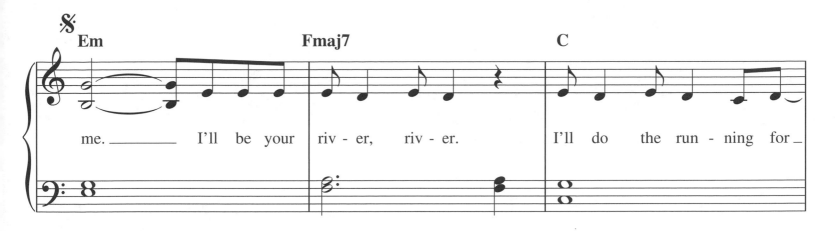

Em / Fmaj7 / C
me. _____ I'll be your riv - er, riv - er. I'll do the run - ning for _

G / Em / Fmaj7
_ you. _ Fol - low me _____ I'll be your riv - er, riv - er.

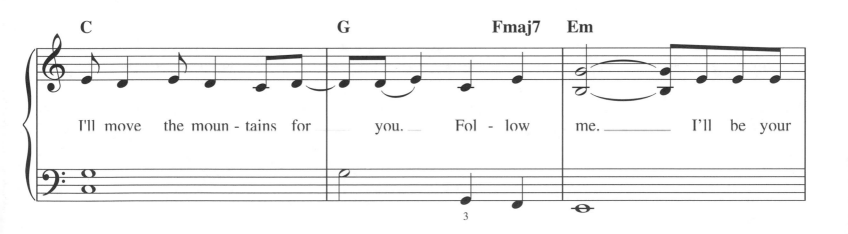

C / G / Fmaj7 Em
I'll move the moun - tains for _ you. _ Fol - low me. _____ I'll be your

Fmaj7 / C / G / Fmaj7
riv - er, riv - er. I'm here to keep you float - ing. _ Fol - low

50

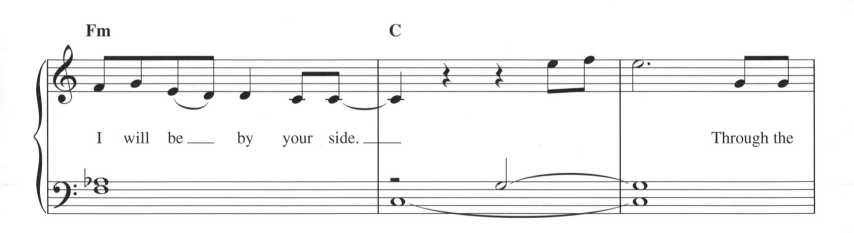

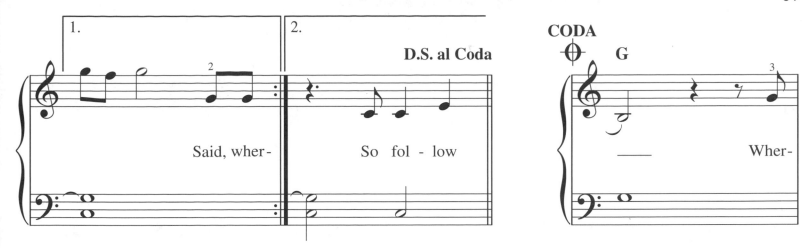

Said, wher- | So fol - low | Wher-

ev - er you're stand - ing | I will be by your side. |

Through the | good, through the bad, I'll | nev - er be hard to

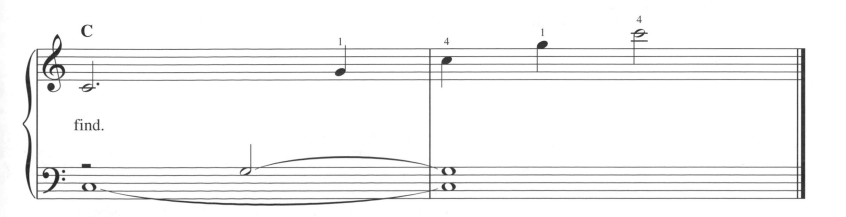

find.

52

LIFETIME

Words and Music by EMELI SANDÉ,
SHAHID KAHN, STEVE MOSTYN,
GLYN AIKINS and LUKE JUBY

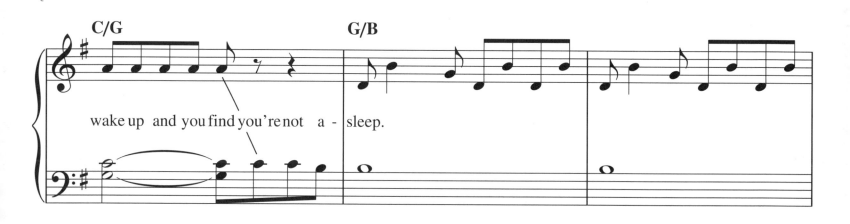

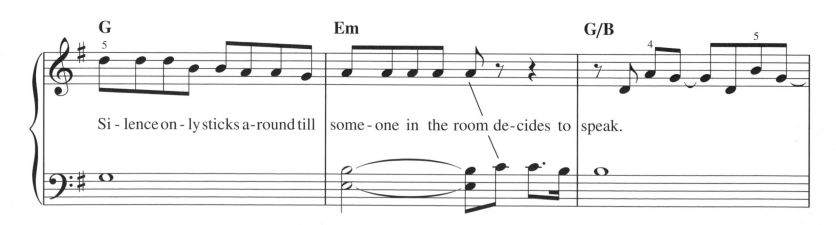

And luck runs out and hearts go cold. We're on-ly young un-til we're old. And

sum-mer leaves us won - drin' where it went. The friends you have can dis-ap-pear. The

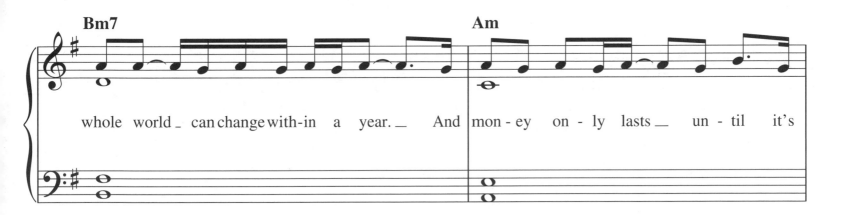

whole world can change with-in a year. And mon-ey on-ly lasts un-til it's

spent. But you, you,

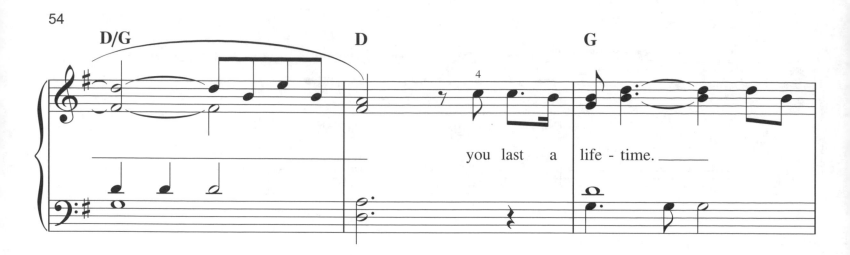

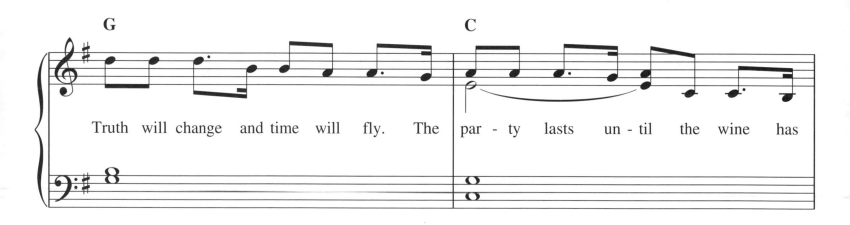

change it's mind and play a dif-f'rent song. We

stay in touch till we for-get. __ And beau-ty fades, the kiss will end. And

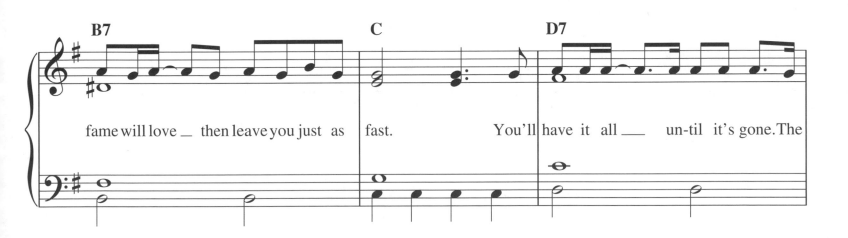

fame will love __ then leave you just as fast. You'll have it all __ un-til it's gone. The

books get burnt and stat-ues fall. Some-times feels like __ noth-ing will ev-er last. _____ But

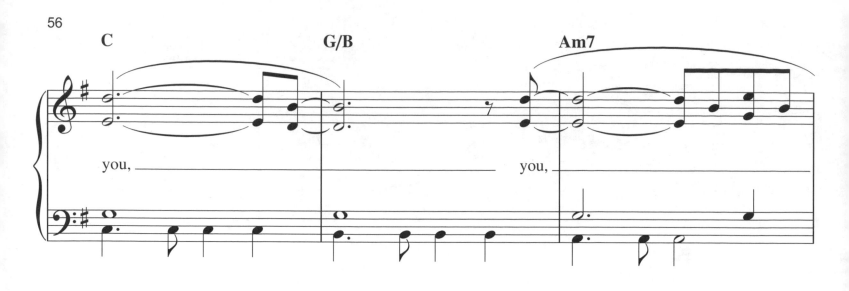

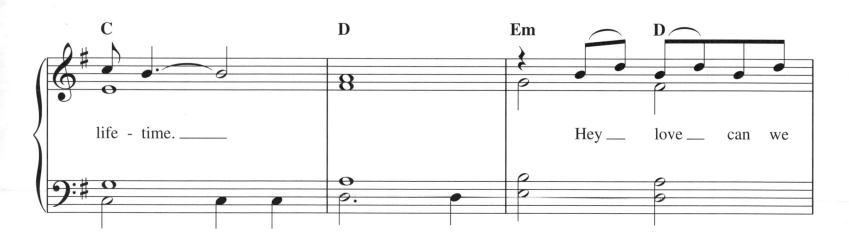

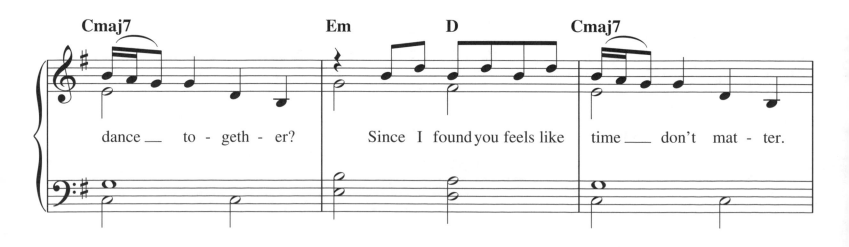

HOPE

Words and Music by EMELI SANDÉ
and ALICIA KEYS

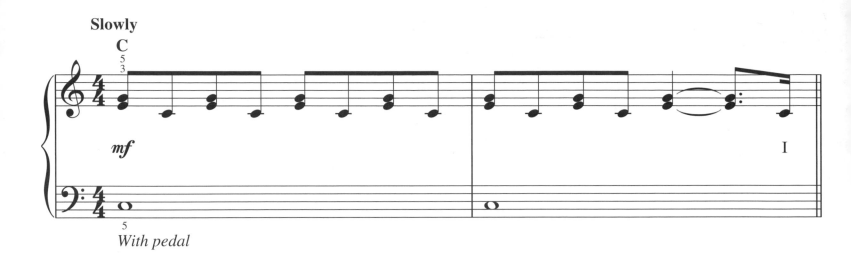

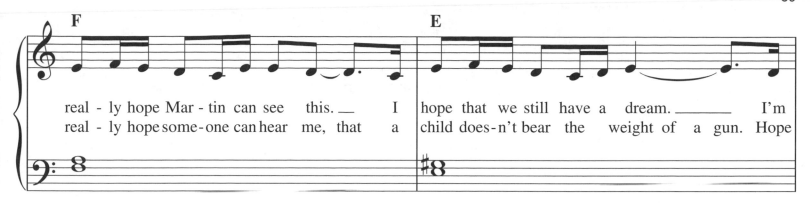

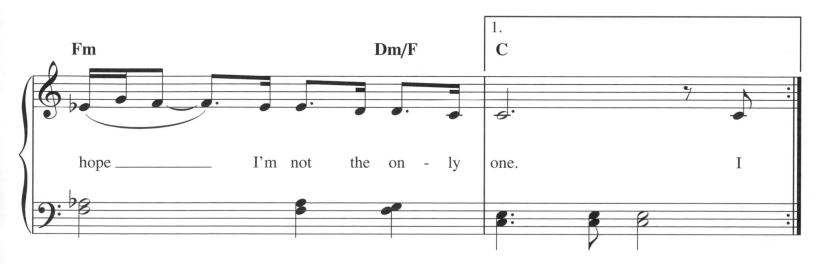

one. Loud - er, _____ I can - not

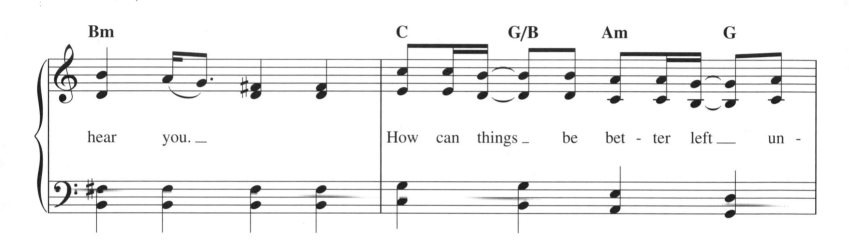

hear you. __ How can things _ be bet - ter left __ un -

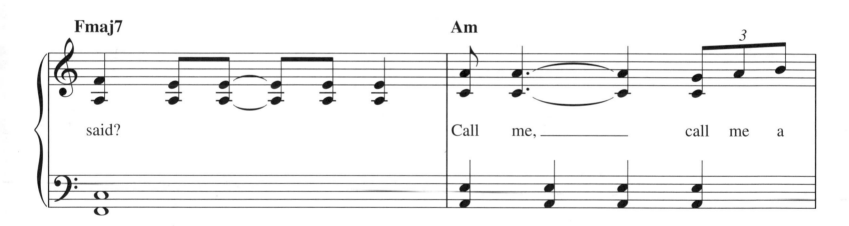

said? Call me, _____ call me a

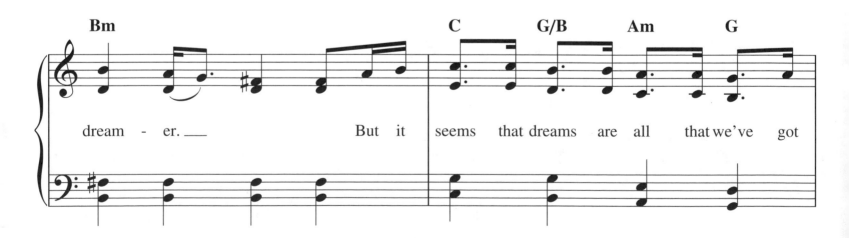

dream - er. __ But it seems that dreams are all that we've got

61

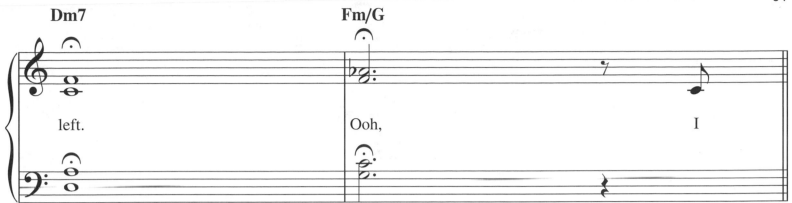

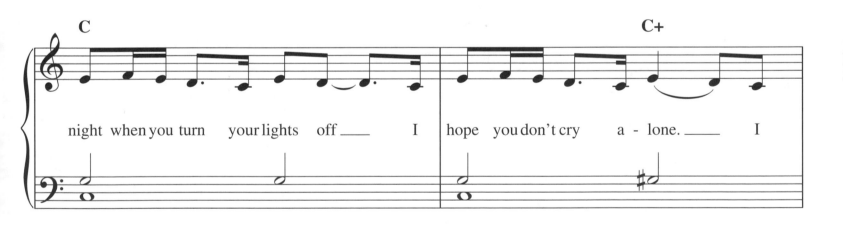

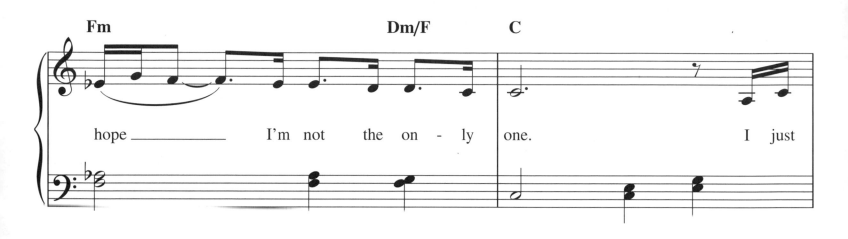

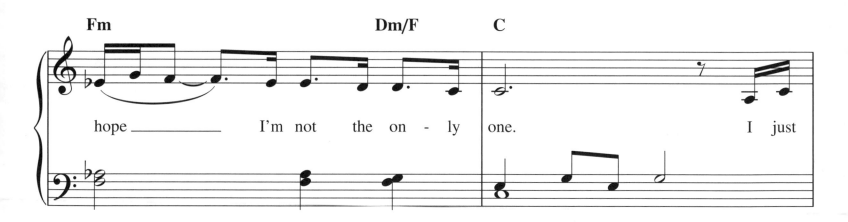

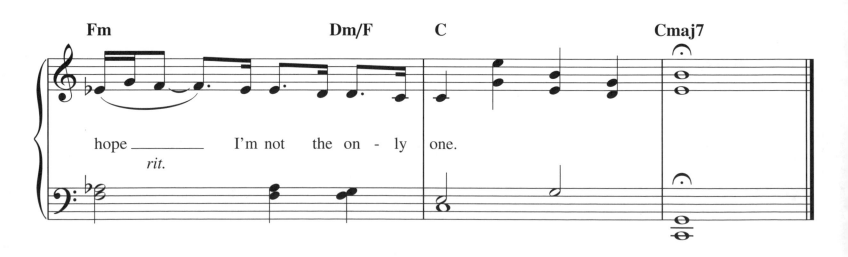

TIGER

Words and Music by EMELI SANDÉ
and SHAHID KHAN

here hold-ing on 'cause I'm tired of grey._ Are you
Bank says I'm poor but I'm feel-in' rich __ if you're
stick-ing a - round. ____

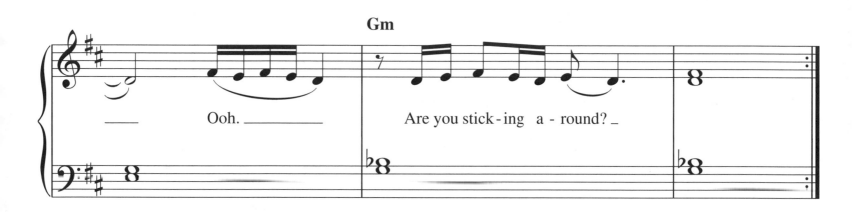

___ Ooh. _____
Are you stick-ing a - round? _

Hey there, __ hon- ey. You came a-long and stopped _ me __ run-ning, __ I'm

mf

feel-ing like _ me, back on my _ feet. I'm a ti-ger a - gain. __

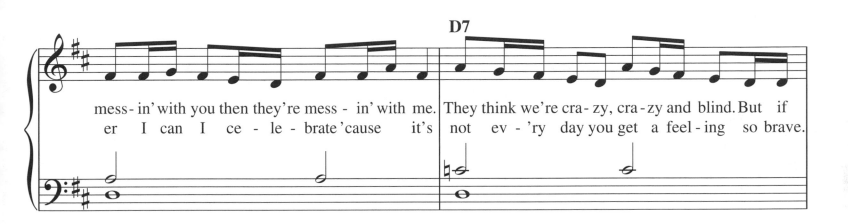

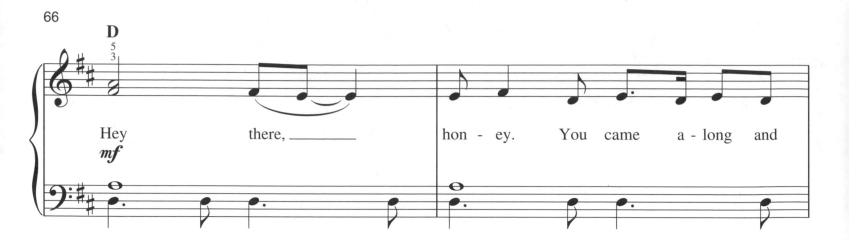

Hey there, _____ hon-ey. You came a-long and

stopped _ me _____ run - ning. _____ I'm

feel - ing like _ me, back on my _ feet. I'm a ti - ger a-

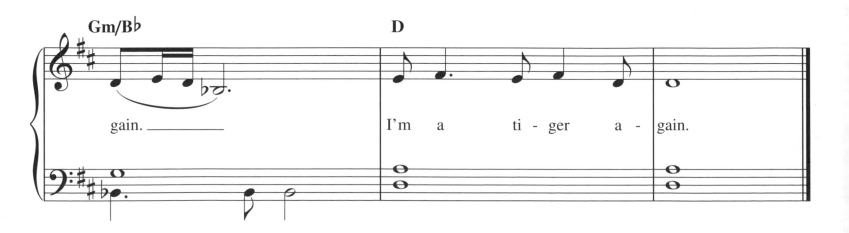

gain. _____ I'm a ti - ger a-gain.

READ ALL ABOUT IT, PART III

Words and Music by EMELI SANDÉ, TOM BARNES,
STEPHEN MANDERSON, IAIN JAMES,
BEN KOHN and PETER KELLEHER

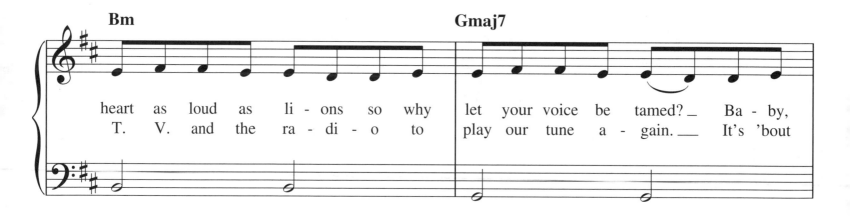

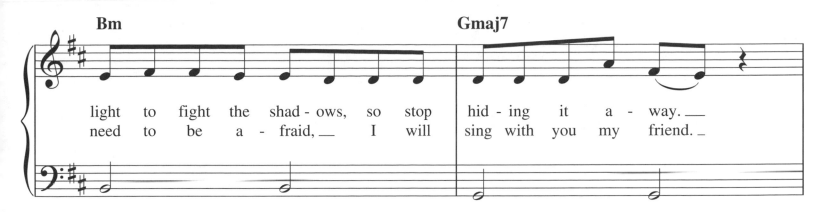

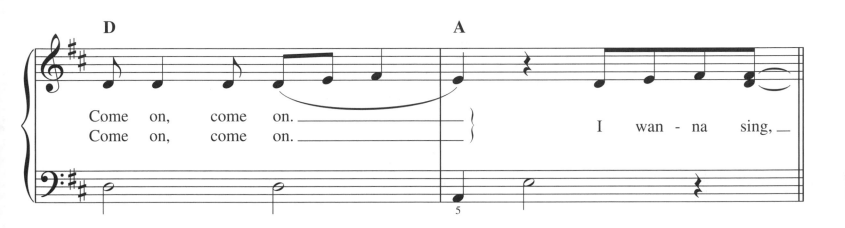

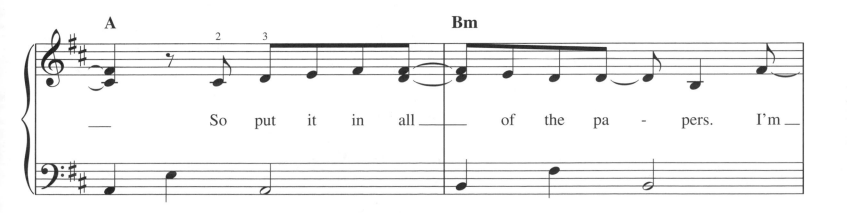

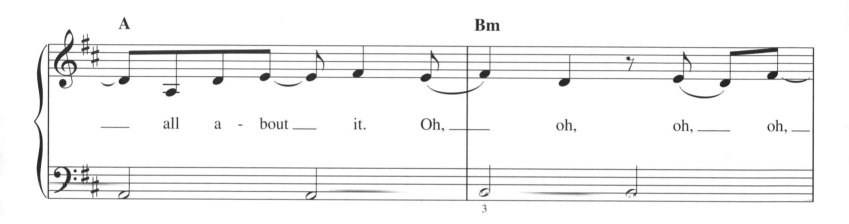

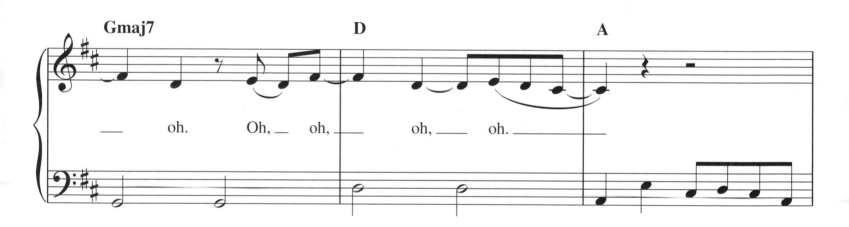

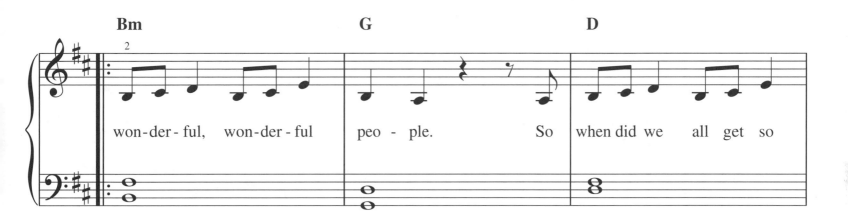

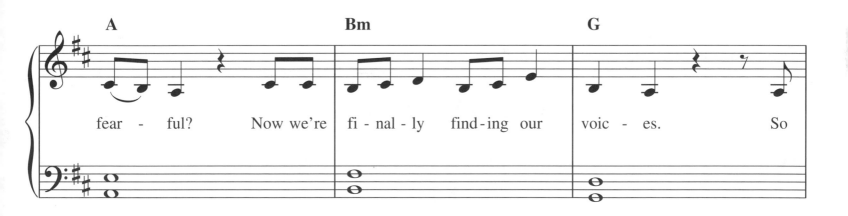

72

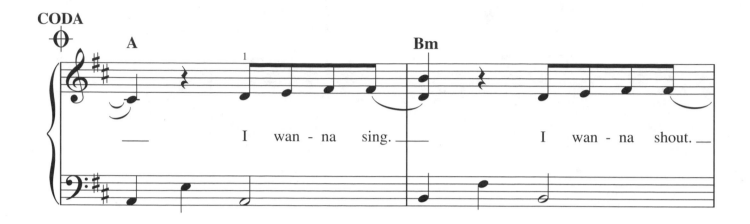

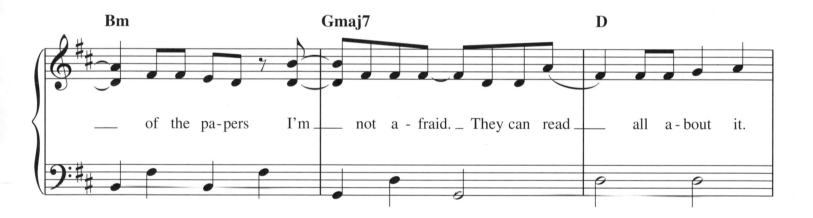

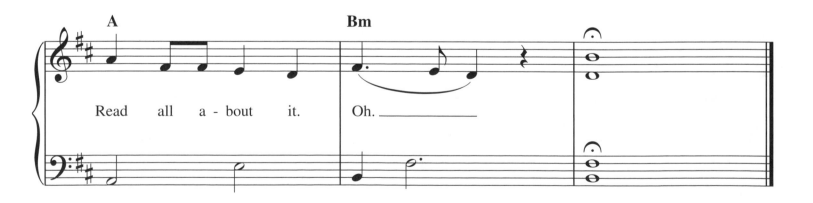